I0004621

Windows 1u

The Practical Step-by-Step Guide to Use Microsoft Windows 10

(Windows for Beginners and Beyond)

Table of Contents

Introduction

Windows 10 was released on July 29th, 2015 as the successor to Windows 8.1. The name Windows "10" is slightly confusing considering there was never a Windows "9", but Microsoft decided to use the number 10 to indicate that this version of Windows will be different. In an attempt to make the OS more like Apple's Mac OSX, Microsoft chose to make Windows 10 have "rolling" (meaning frequent but small) updates. What this means is that there will probably never be a Windows 11, just as there will probably not be an OSXI. Rather, updates will increase functionality to Windows 10 over time but the core operating system will stay the same.

Many people upgraded to Windows 10 within the first year because it was offered for free to anyone with a copy of Windows 7 or 8. Additionally, the number of people that took advantage of this offer was substantial- probably in large part to the public's distaste for Windows 8. The free upgrade period has since closed, but Windows 10 still comes for free on most new computer purchases.

Microsoft decided to do away with many of the problems that plagued Windows 8, and thus Windows 10 most resembles Windows 7 in aesthetics and functionality. The classic start menu has returned, apps have been integrated better, and there is more of a balance between "metro" and "legacy". Now most of this probably doesn't make sense if you haven't fully experienced Windows 7, 8, and 8.1, but essentially Windows 10 is offering a huge improvement over the older operating systems. If you are fully lost with the jargon, the "Windows Basics" section in this book will get you started.

Whether you updated to 10 by accident, bought a new computer with it preinstalled, or updated to get away from Windows 8, Windows 10 can offer you plenty of great uses. The

OS is now relatively faster, more secure, more user-friendly, and full of new features that help you connect with the world. This book hopes to help you on your way to discovering Windows 10.

How to Upgrade to Windows 10 on PC

The free upgrade period for Windows 10 expired on July 29th, 2016, and with it, the easiest way to upgrade is gone as well. Previously there was a button that you could press to upgrade your computer automatically, but that button has since disappeared and the upgrade process has changed.

There are a few different methods that you can take to upgrade, but they will cost money considering the free upgrade is over. You can:

1. Buy a new computer with Windows 10 preinstalled. Windows 10 is essentially "free", but you still have to pay a substantial cost for a new computer. This is only recommended if your computer is failing or severely out of date.
2. Buy a Windows 10 upgrade disc. You may be able to find a disc at a retailer such as BestBuy with which you can upgrade your system. This method is recommended because you will not have to download too many files and it will generally run faster, provided you have a DVD drive on your computer to run it!
3. Buy the Windows 10 upgrade download. From Microsoft's website you can pay for a Windows 10 download. This will instantly start retrieving all the files needed to upgrade, but it could be terribly slow on a bad internet connection.
4. Pay somebody to upgrade your computer for you. Some services, such as Geek Squad or likely any local

computer business can upgrade your computer for you-at a price of course. While this is certainly the easiest method, the prices that 3rd parties charge can be very high.

Anyhow, if you pay for the download or buy the disc, you will then need to start the upgrade. For discs, place the DVD into the tray, close it, and wait for any on-screen prompts. For downloads, wait for the file to finish downloading and then launch the upgrade file by double clicking it. At this point, both methods should converge. You need to confirm the on-screen prompts and follow the directions in the upgrade. Windows will ask you a few questions, such as if you would like to keep your data or start with a fresh new installation. You know best what option you would like to choose, but for reference, most people would like to keep their programs and files and just upgrade the operating system.

In a few rare cases, some programs that you have installed may be incompatible with Windows 10. In this case, the upgrade will not commence but rather it will inform you of the complication and give you directions on how to solve the issue. If the issue is too complicated, definitely consider paying a 3rd party to have your computer updated.

Nonetheless, follow all on-screen prompts, make relevant choices, and eventually the upgrade process will start. It usually takes about 90 minutes to 2 hours, so make sure you have the time to spare. If you own a laptop, plug it in so the battery will not die.

Windows will finish upgrading, and you will have a brand new operating system to play with. There are plenty of new features that this book will explain, so have fun with it. One interesting thing to note is that you CAN revert the upgrade to your previous version of Windows within the first month if you do not like Windows 10. We will discuss that more in the FAQs, but don't be disheartened if the screen looks different or objects are not in the same place they were. Honestly, Windows 10 is an improvement over other versions; it just might take some time to get used to.

How to Upgrade a Windows Phone to Windows 10

Upgrading your phone to Windows 10 is actually much easier than upgrading a PC. Some phones are shipping with the new OS preinstalled, but most of the phones need to be updating manually. The update is available for nearly all Windows phones that run the 8.1 mobile operating system; to check and see if your phone can be upgraded, install the "upgrade advisor" app from the store and run it. The app should tell you if your phone is ready to upgrade. If you get the all-clear, you need to go to your settings app, then tap on the "phone update" tab, then "check for updates". Be sure to do this on Wi-Fi, otherwise the large download will use up all of your mobile data.

The phone will retrieve the Windows 10 download and then ask you if it should install. Confirm, make sure your phone is plugged in, and then let it do the upgrade. The whole process might take an hour or so- your phone will be unusable during this time. There also may be some additional on-screen prompts that you need to confirm, but eventually, your phone will be upgraded to Windows 10. Specific apps need to be upgraded too, but this process is automatic and may take some time. If all of your personal apps are not showing, just note that Windows 10 will put them back after it finishes upgrading them.

The best part about Windows 10 for phones is that it can run many of the same applications that Windows 10 can. Most everything downloaded from the Windows store is cross-compatible between the two devices. Additionally, there are some extra features available through Windows 10's "phone companion" that will be discussed later in the book.

Windows Basics

For your first time starting your computer or logging into the OS, Windows will guide you through what you need to do to get set up. Just follow along with the prompts until it gives you actual control over your computer. The first thing you will see is your desktop. This isn't to be confused with the type of computer you have- laptops and desktops. Rather the entirety of your screen is the "desktop", and that is how you interact with your computer. You can control the PC with the keyboard and mouse. The mouse is used to move the white arrow "pointer" across the screen, and you "click" by pressing the left button down. Refer to the picture below for explanations of assorted screen items.

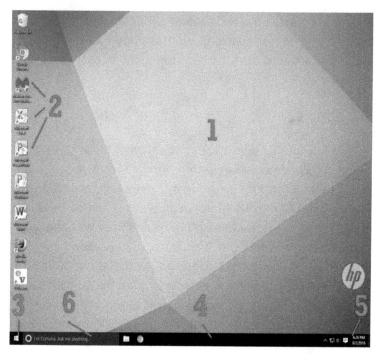

1 – Desktop – Everything on the screen is the desktop.

2 – Icons – The small pictures, such as those shown for number 2 are icons. Icons can be files, folders, or programs. You can open any icon by "double clicking" or clicking twice fast in succession on the icon. Files are pieces of data such as documents, a song, or an email. Folders are containers that hold other icons. Programs, or applications, or apps, are interactive pieces of software that let you achieve a task such as checking your email, browsing the web, or listening to music.

3 - Start Button – The start button is how you "start" most things on your computer. You can click on it to open up the "start menu" from which you can open various programs or interact with your PC.

4 - Task Bar – The task bar shows any open files, folders, and programs by exhibiting its icon. The two icons in the picture above are not actually open; they are "shortcuts" that can be clicked on to quickly open any of those two programs. When you actually have things running on your computer, you can see them appear in the task bar.

5 – Tray – A small corner of your screen that has quick links to commonly changed options such as time, volume, and more.

6 - Cortana Search Bar – A new feature in Windows 10, you can click on number 6 to search your computer or the internet. We'll talk more about this later.

Starting an application, file, or folder is as easy as double-clicking it, or searching for it through the start menu and clicking it there. Throughout this book, we will "open" programs, apps, and so forth and this is what is meant by it.

The purpose of computers is to utilize the applications available to you to achieve your goals. Whether you wish to keep in contact with friends and family, or whether you need to use a computer for work, Windows 10 provides methods to you. It is highly recommended that you practice with your computer before continuing in the book. This section was dedicated to an absolute beginner, but the rest of the book can help those that know a small bit about computers and Windows 7/8, but not a lot about Windows 10. To learn more about how your computer works, do not be afraid to explore the preinstalled programs. Click the start button and try out everything you see to really get a grasp on how computers work. And if you get stumped, you can always ask a friend or family member for help.

New and Improved Features for Windows 10

1. Improved start menu

It is no doubt that many Windows 8 and 8.1 users absolutely hated the "metro" start menu replacing the classic look of Windows 7's menu. In fact, it is not surprising that most people took advantage of the free upgrade period just to ditch the tablet-style user interface from 8. Ultimately, 8's mess of a start menu was a mistake on Microsoft's part that they intended to fix in later versions of Windows. Thus the Windows 10 hybrid-style menu is born.

The start menu in 10 is optimized for both desktops and tablets. The classic menu returns on the left side, while the metro-style app buttons are integrated tastefully on the right. By clicking the start button in the lower left-hand corner (or by tapping the Windows button on the keyboard), the start menu will open. You may refer to the picture excerpt below.

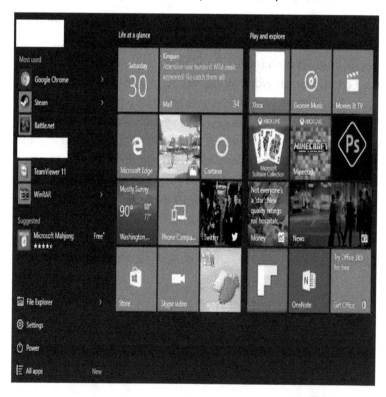

Notice that there are recently used applications on the left ala Windows 7, while Windows 8-type apps are launch-able on the right partition. Every part of the screen is customizable, so if you want to remove an app or program from a list, just right click on the item to see more options.

2. Search features

It may not be obvious from the previous screenshot, but the start menu has built-in search functionality just as previous versions of Windows did. To access this feature, just begin typing while the start menu is open. In the picture below, I have started typing "Internet..." and the computer has searched the computer to show the results visible. This can work with folders and files too so if you are looking for pictures, try typing "pictures".

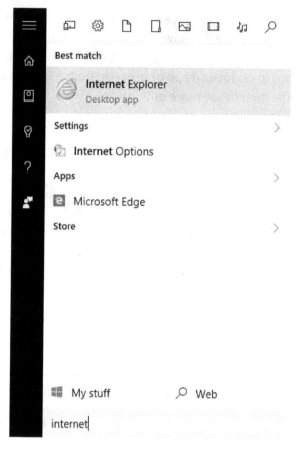

Search is expanded in Windows 10 to include additional functionality- Cortana. Cortana makes searching the computer easy and natural, mostly because you can use your voice. Just like Amazon's Alexa and Apple's Siri, Microsoft's Cortana is a full-fledged personal digital assistant. You can ask Cortana to give you news, find information online, set timers, and much more. Under the "ask me anything" section of the start bar, click the microphone icon to ask Cortana a question. You can use natural English to speak to Cortana as a person, and she will translate your words into tasks and perform them.

3. Virtual Desktops

Other operating systems, such as those based on Linux, have had multiple "virtual" desktops for years. This refers to the fact that you can simulate having more than one screen for productivity reasons. For example, you can have music playing on one virtual desktop screen while typing an email on the other. The process to create or remove virtual desktops is quick and easy, plus it will save you time in the long run with ease of multitasking.

To create a virtual desktop, you will need to navigate to and then click the "Task view" button (it is by default directly to the right of the search button on the taskbar). Alternatively, you can use the keyboard shortcut Win+Tab to enter task view. Task view is also a helpful new feature that enumerates all open windows on your screen and allows you to select which one you want to make active. Creating the virtual desktop now is as simple as clicking the plus button on the right of the screen. You can now switch between your virtual desktops through task view. Definitely try increasing the speed of your workflow by partitioning tasks between virtual desktops.

4. The Action Center

With larger app store integration comes features common in mobile devices and Apple computers – notifications. Notifications are alerts coming from your apps, such as new emails, new instant messages, weather alerts, and much more. These notifications be viewed through the action center, an all-new feature that gives quick links to various options. Action center is opened by clicking the speech bubble looking icon on the bottom right of the taskbar or through the keyboard shortcut Win+A. It appears on the right side of the screen and presents new notifications for you to view. By clicking on a notification, you can learn more or access the app it comes from. And to clear the notifications click the "clear all" button at the very top-right. Probably the most powerful quick link in the action center is the "all settings" button, which launches the "settings" app where you can adjust just about every setting of Windows.

5. Tablet Integration (that works)

While Windows 8 frustrated users by predicting everyone would be using the OS on a tablet, Windows 10 understands that many of us are using laptops and desktops that are much more comfortably operated while using the classic interface.

However, tablet-type functionality is still present and actually improved upon. You can find a unique feature, tablet mode, through the action center. By clicking the tablet mode button, you change Windows 10's interface slightly to be more comfortable on touch screen computers. This maximizes the active window and increases the size of buttons.

Tablet mode is started automatically with Windows 10's "continuum", which changes between modes when "transformable" computers are docked or undocked from a keyboard. Office workers can now have a work desk set up with speakers, multiple monitors, and their keyboard. While mobile or on-site somewhere their device can function as a touch screen tablet, and as they return to their desk, they can dock the tablet and have it transform into a laptop or desktop. Microsoft's Surface line of computers is great for this feature because they work with and without the dock-able keyboard.

6. Snap

Snap is a feature that was present in both Windows 7 and 8, but evolving technology has brought us bigger monitors with more screen real estate. While we could previously only snap left and right, on Windows 10 we can snap applications in all 4 corners to make full use of every bit of space. Just as with regular snap, the method to achieve this is to drag a program by its top bar and put it into a corner. The transparent guide lines will indicate that it will snap into a corner, and then you can let go. Placing multiple windows in different parts of the screen neatly is a great way to look at two things at once, compare windows, or to read one thing while typing into another.

7.   Smartphone integration

A new feature that is sure to appeal to those that are on-the-go is smartphone integration. Firstly, certain Windows phones can upgrade to a mobile version of Windows 10 that retains many features of the desktop version (as we have discussed before). For example, you can use the same store app on either device and they will perform basically the same. If you sign in to both with the same account, you can even share files and other data between the two platforms.

Another great smartphone feature is the shared Action Center. Action center will be synced between all Windows devices you are signed into, so if you get a text message on your phone, it will also notify you on your desktop. Or if you get a desktop notification away from home, the phone will display the same message. At the time, actually, you don't even necessarily need a Windows brand phone for rudimentary smartphone integration, as iOS and Android phones can access their own set of integration features. To do this, you need to start the Phone companion app from your Windows 10 computer. This will be explained more fully in the section about apps.

Keyboard Shortcuts in Windows 10

Windows 10 comes with increased functionality, so Microsoft decided to include more keyboard shortcuts as well. You might think that using the mouse to complete actions in a familiar way is easier and faster, but you would be missing out on a serious productivity tool by skipping keyboard shortcuts. Once you learn of alternative ways to accomplish your tasks, you will inevitably speed up your entire computing experience. Keyboard shortcuts do not need to be pressed simultaneously; rather they should be pressed one at a time while continuing to hold the previous buttons. For this reason, you usually need two hands to perform keyboard shortcuts.

First, we will discuss common keyboard shortcuts that were available in previous versions of Windows, and then we will talk about shortcuts exclusive and new to Windows 10.

Some of the keyboard conventions are listed below:

Win = Windows Key		
Alt = Alternate	Alt	
Ctrl = Control	Ctrl	
Shift	⇧ Shift	
Up	↑	
Down	↓	
Left	←	

Right	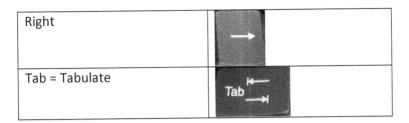
Tab = Tabulate	

Common Windows shortcuts

Ctrl+Alt+Del

Change to a menu that offers additional functionality. People usually use this menu to access Task Manager, or they use it when their computer has locked up.

Ctrl+Shift+Escape

Open Task Manager directly. With Task Manager you can close unresponsive applications with the "End Task" button.

Windows+L

Lock your screen and require your password to unlock. This is helpful for when you need to leave your computer unattended with other people around.

Alt+Tab

Switch between open programs. By just pressing Alt+Tab, you will switch to the next open program. By continuing to hold alt while tapping tab multiple times, you can select exactly which program you are switching to. This is definitely the greatest time saver for those that switch between programs often.

Ctrl+C

Copies the selected text.

Ctrl+X

Cuts the selected text. Cutting is just copying, but it removes the text in the process.

Ctrl+V

Pastes the selected text. You might wonder why we use V instead of P. See below.

Ctrl+P

Print the active selection. Doing this in Microsoft Word, for example, will print the current document. Doing this on a webpage on the internet will print out the website.

Ctrl+B, U, I

Bolds, underlines, or italicizes the selected text. These key combinations only work in specific applications, such as Microsoft Office products or while typing an email in a web browser.

Ctrl+Z

Undo. This will do away with whatever action you have just performed. Accidently deleted a file? Undo will put it back. Typed a bland sentence? Undo will get rid of it. It has a history limit, though, so it can't fix things that happened too long ago. Additionally, it will start with the most recent action and undo it, so Ctrl+Z is only really useful directly after your mistake.

Ctrl+Y

Redo. This redoes and undo you just did. While that was a very confusing line, the command itself isn't nearly as confusing. For example, if you write a bad paragraph and decide to get rid of it through undo, redo can put it back when you change your mind. Undo and redo are most helpful in Microsoft Office products.

Win+F

Start a search

Win+R

Open the "Run" application.

Alt+F4

Close the currently active program.

And here are a few keyboard shortcuts that are new to Windows 10.

Win+Tab

Open Task View. Much easier than trying to find the button on the taskbar.

Win+C

Open Cortana. Use this keyboard shortcut with a microphone for ultimate efficiency; you'll never even need to use your mouse! If you don't have a microphone, use Win+S instead so you can type.

Win+A

Open Action Center.

Win+Up/Down/Left/Right

Snap active window to the direction provided. Do it a second time to snap to a corner.

Win+Ctrl+D

Create a new virtual desktop.

Win+Ctrl+Left/Right

Switch between Virtual Desktops.

Win+I

Open the settings application.

Essential Apps for Windows 10

Windows 8 introduced a new way to download programs - the Windows Store. This divided programs into two distinct categories - Store Apps and Legacy Apps. Windows 10 improved upon their store apps for the "Universal" apps we have now- universal meaning they can work on any Windows 10 device. Store apps are downloaded from the store and have to be reviewed by Microsoft before being published. Legacy apps are the programs that can be downloaded from the internet as .exe files and run normally. Store apps are much safer, because they are reviewed and have a set of standards to pass before being made available. Legacy programs have the potential of containing malware and viruses, but that's how we have downloaded new programs for a long time now.

While legacy programs will never completely leave, store apps are amazingly useful and easy to obtain. By starting the Windows Store application, you can search for new apps or browse through popular ones. Starting individual apps is as easy as searching through the start menu or clicking a live tile.

Here are a few essential apps that come with Windows 10:

Weather

One of the most used apps on my devices would be the weather. After starting this app for the first time, you select your preferences and enter your city. If you have a GPS installed (such as in your phone), you can have it auto-detect your location. The app can then start proper and do what it is meant to do- show you the weather! In addition to the forecast, you can also view the radar map, historical data, and the day's news. While this is a relatively simple app, it comes in handy on numerous occasions.

Calendar

The calendar is more than just a calendar, as this app can act as a personal agenda for you and your engagements. Starting the app will prompt it to ask you for an account. By linking an account, you can share your to-do list and events across multiple devices. Cortana integration with Calendar is strong, for you can say something like "add my appointment to the doctor for tomorrow at noon to the calendar" and Cortana will schedule your event.

Calculator

While Calculator is a simple app, it can save you time and desk space so you can do away with your dedicated calculator. With a full keyboard, the number pad on the right serves as a mini-keypad for the calculator. It is definitely hand for quick arithmetic and saves time over pencil and paper.

Camera

For laptops and desktops with webcams, the camera app provides access to your peripheral. On a phone, the camera app is useful for taking pictures. On a PC the camera app is useful as a mirror or for webchats. See Skype below for using your camera to talk to friends, family, or for a job meeting.

Mail

Even though you probably already check your mail through a web browser, the mail app can simplify the process exponentially. You can sign into multiple mail accounts and have them all arrive at the same location. Furthermore, Windows 10's notifications can alert you when you get an email from any one of your email addresses. No longer will you have to press the refresh button over and over on multiple websites, for you can now wait for the mail to come to you.

Maps

Just like Google Maps or MapQuest, Microsoft's Maps can show you a street map of any location. You can type in your address to see your local map, or type in a remote location to see its map. In some big cities, there is a street view mode that allows you to see an area as if you were standing there. This is helpful for locating landmarks when traveling to a new area. If you need directions between two places, maps can do that for you too. You even have the option of printing out a step by step guide on how to get to a location.

Edge

News

The News app has multiple ways of delivering news to you. You can see global headlines when starting the app, or you can input your location for local news in another tab. If you teach the app some of your favorite news categories, it will begin showing you more relevant news to your tastes.

People

People is definitely a useful app provided you are using the other apps in this list. People acts as a contact list where you can store your friends, family, and co-workers. Then, you can quickly contact any of the people in your address book through any other application in which you provided their information for. For example, if you put their phone number, it will call them. If you provided an email, it would start composing a new email to them. So the best uses from people come if you also use the other apps on this list.

Phone Companion

Possibly the best app on this list, Phone Companion allows your Windows 10 computer and cell phone to communicate for increased functionality. Although every feature is available to those with Windows 10 phone, you may also use your Android or iOS phone with Phone Companion. After starting the app, it will give you directions on how to connect your devices together. Windows phones are a breeze to connect, but other devices may need a separate application downloaded. Now your contact, OneNote, Skype, Office, email, calendar, photos, and Cortana can be shared across your devices. New functionality is added all the time, so there may be even more cross-compatibility in the future.

Settings

This is the same settings application that can be accessed through the Action Center. Settings offer one place to edit most every Windows setting on your computer. If you need to change something, always check here.

Sports

Sports works much in the same way that News does, as it allows you to see the biggest sports news, check how your favorite teams are doing, or look at scores live as the games are going on. Sports is definitely an app for the sports fan.

Xbox

For the gamer, the Xbox app can sufficiently fulfill your guilty pleasure. The Xbox app can let you play all sorts of entertaining games, connect with a community of gamers, or learn the newest news in the digital world. If you have kids with an Xbox One console, you can connect it to your device to play gorgeous games right on your computer.

Store

The store is an app you use to get more apps. Microsoft offers the store as a portal to over half a million apps, some free and some paid. Just about everything you can think of could possibly be in the store, and the slogan "there's an app for that" surely comes to mind. You can search by typing in an app's name or subject in the search box.

Edge

Users of other Microsoft operating systems will remember Internet Explorer. Whether you loved it or hated it, Internet Explorer has almost been completely replaced by Edge. Edge aims to fix everything wrong with IE by removing the bloat that kept IE slow and clunky. There are new features included in the edge, such as Cortana integration, fast page loading, and more secure options. Edge could possibly be the first app you use in Windows 10, so give it a try and see if you like it. If it is just too complicated or unusual for you, check below for some app recommendation that can replace Edge.

Apps You Must Download from the Store

The included apps are great, but the best ones are the Apps you can download. These apps below are the ones I couldn't do without on a new computer. Most are also free so you can download them right now.

Skype

Skype is an app that you can use to call or instant message people. On a phone or laptop, it can take advantage of your webcam so you can video chat as well. The app is free, but you can pay money for credits that allow you to make long distance calls around the world. Most people have this installed on their computer and phone, so it is an easy way to stay in touch.

Office

Microsoft's Office suite is the de facto set of software for writing documents, making PowerPoints, editing spreadsheets, and other common "office" tasks. It has become an industry standard and is used just about everywhere. The problem is that Office is not particularly free. The price ranges, but it is well worth it for any individual that does a lot of document creation. Office includes Word, PowerPoint, Excel, and Publisher usually. Other products in Office are OneNote and Access.

OneNote

If you are a busy person, or perhaps a forgetful one, then Microsoft's OneNote could help you significantly. The app does just what the title suggests; OneNote saves text "notes" for later. It is a good program for jotting down quick ideas or grocery lists, as the lists can be synced across devices. One decent tactic for its use involves taking notes while going through the fridge, and then pulling up the shopping list when you're at the store. Other features include a pen that you can use to scribble actual notes, a feature perfect for touchscreen devices.

Chrome/Firefox

While Edge performs admirably, every person has their own internet browser preference. Alternative browsers, such as Google Chrome and Mozilla Firefox, are popular because of their different approaches. For example, Chrome is known for being fast and compatible, while Firefox is known for being customizable and secure. Definitely, download an alternative browser and try surfing the internet. The small things, such as the way Firefox scrolls smoothly or how Chrome is lightning fast on some websites can make you choose one over the other.

Windows Media Player/Spotify/iTunes

Your computer can be used for music too. If you have an audio CD, put it on your desktop or laptop, and you will be greeted with a few options. Opening the CD in Windows Media Player will begin playing your CD right off the bat. If you own an iPhone, iPod, or iPad, then Apple's iTunes is the piece of software you will need to do certain things with your mobile device. You can install iTunes and play CDs through it as well. But CDs are getting phased out in the modern age in favor of digital music. Music can be bought and downloaded through iTunes, but most people prefer to stream music for free. Streaming means that the music is downloaded as you listen to it and then deleted right after so you don't fill up your hard drive space. Spotify comes out on top as the best music streamer. With Spotify, you can search for specific artists, songs, or albums to play from, or you can give control to the application and let it choose what to play for you. Overall Spotify is the best choice for listening to music without buying every song you want to hear.

Dropbox

Many of us use additional computers and mobile devices, so sharing files across them is extremely difficult.

Dropbox aims to fix that by offering an app that can "sync" your files automatically between all of your devices with dropbox installed. Here's an example: you may be working on a letter in Microsoft Word that you want to take with you to work. If you have Dropbox installed, save it to the Dropbox folder and head on to work. When you get there, the file will automatically also be in your work computer's Dropbox folder as well. This applies to phones with it installed too so that you can share any file between devices on the go and without any additional setup.

The Photos App

For many, the photos app is the most used and useful on Windows 10. Computers are amazing because of the vast amount of storage space gained through digitizing items, so it is no doubt that converting a giant album of photos down to the size of a pin is extremely helpful.

The Windows 10 Photos app is relatively easy to use, but we will expand upon its use here. When the app is first started, you will likely be greeted by a few of your pictures on the "collection" tab. Collection initially shows your photos organized by date. You can scroll up and down this windows to see your photos, or click on a specific one to get a closer look. If you don't have any photos on your computer, but rather you have them on your phone or digital camera, you can click the Import button at the top to bring them in. Import looks like an arrow pointing down into a square, and by clicking it, the app will prompt you to select the device to import from. Make sure you've plugged your camera device into the computer beforehand, and it will show up in this window. After confirming the correct device, your pictures will be transferred to your computer.

The 2nd tab, albums, is one way to group your photos into picture books. Initially, Windows 10 will attempt to categorize your pictures for you, but you most likely have specific ideas on where you want your pictures to go. So by clicking the plus button at the top, you can create new picture albums to sort your pictures into.

Everybody has a certain way they download photos. For example, some people download their photos and sort them into the "pictures" folder on Windows, while others get their photos from the internet and keep them in the "Downloads" folder. Either way, the photos app can pull from multiple locations on a computer, which is what the "folders" tab does. It will automatically contain your "pictures" folder and maybe even your "OneDrive" folder, but feel free to click "choose source folders for photos and videos" to specify more locations to pull from. Admittedly it is fairly hard to keep a neat and organized computer, so the photos app does most of the hard work for you by organizing your collection and presenting it to you in a clear way.

Conclusively, Windows 10's Photos app is a fantastic addition to your computer. While locating and presenting pictures was decently tough in previous versions, Windows 10 makes it easy to grow your collection of photographs and videos.

Windows 10 FAQ

Windows 10 is a new and confusing system at times. Options that you previously knew how to change might be in a different place now, or you might be confused about how to achieve certain tasks. This frequently asked questions section can maybe help you with any problem you come across.

Q: Is there any way to get my old version of Windows back?

A: Within the first month of installation, yes, you can revert back to your old version of Windows. This is only applicable if you "upgraded" from Windows 7/8. If you got a new computer or erased all the data off of your old one to install Windows 10 than you have erased the older version of Windows as well. To start the downgrade process, open the "Settings" app either by searching or from the Action Center. In the "Update & Security" tab, select "recovery". If you indeed did an upgrade and it was within the past month, you will see an option to "go back" to your previous version of Windows. Click on it to begin the downgrade.

Q: I see many different versions of Windows 10, such as Home, Pro, and Enterprise. Which do I need?

A: Unless you are in a business, you will not need an enterprise edition of Windows. For the vast majority of users, Windows will be upgrading you to the version that matches your previous version of Windows. So if you previously had a home edition of Windows 7/8, you will be upgraded to the home edition of Windows 10. In case you are purchasing your upgrade as a disc or download, though, you can choose which version to install. In short- Home should contain every feature you need, while Pro is more for the "power user". Pro contains a few features that Home does not, such as remote desktop, App Locker, and Active Directory. Unless you specifically need a special feature of Pro edition, Home edition will definitely suffice.

Q: I am happy with my current Windows OS, do I absolutely need to upgrade to Windows 10?

A: While Windows 10 offers many advanced features and improvements, it is not for everybody. If your computer is too slow currently and barely can run its current version of Windows, you might not want to upgrade. If you love your current layout and computing experience, Windows 10 might interrupt your "flow". In short- you do not NEED to upgrade, but please note that Windows 7 will stop receiving security patches in 2020. When that time comes, yes you NEED to upgrade to Windows 10. Between now and then, though, the choice is up to you. I highly recommend upgrading, however, because of the security improvements and new features that Windows 10 offers.

Q: How do I open "app-name-here"?

A: If you can't find an app, file, or folder that you know you have on your computer, press the start button and type the name in. It will search your computer and display relevant results.

Q: Do I have to use apps from the Windows Store?

A: Not at all. If you have your own favorite legacy programs, you can continue to use them. Windows Apps are just an easier way to add functionality to your computer.

Q: How do I change the way things work?

A: Through the "Settings" app. Search for it or start it from the Action Center.

Q: Where are my files?

A: For the most part Windows tries to sort your files into relevant folders. This means that pictures are likely to be in the "pictures" folder, music may be in "music, and so on. Search for these folders to open them. If you upgraded to Windows 10 from a different version, your previous files should still be where you left them.

Q: How do I connect to Wi-Fi?

A: On the desktop, check the Tray in the bottom right-hand corner for the connect icon.

Q: How do I "insert-anything-here"?

A: If you have a specific action you want to take but you don't know how, the internet can be your best friend. Google specifically is a great place to ask questions. First, open up an internet browser and navigate to http://www.google.com. Type in your question into the search box and Google will give you links to websites that might have your answer.

Conclusion

Windows 10 doesn't have to be difficult. It might look very different than what we are used to, but it surely brings many benefits to those who upgrade. The new apps, keyboard shortcuts, and features allow you to accomplish so much more with your devices.

And while this book is very helpful, it can never cover every topic you might need help with. Google is a fantastic way to find information, and that applies to help questions as well. By experimenting around with Windows 10 and getting help where you need it, eventually, you will master the software.

Thank you for taking the time to read this book, and I hope it was able to answer a few of the beginner questions that you had about Windows 10.